POSY EDWARDS

MILEY CYRUS: ME & YOU

STAR OF HANNAH MONTANA

Miley!

Full name: Born Destiny Hope Cyrus now changed legally to Miley Ray Cyrus

Nickname: Smiley then shortened to Miley, sometimes her dad calls her Mile

Birthday: 23 November 1992

Age: 15

Sign: Sagittarius

Chinese horoscope sign: The monkey

Favourite author: Roald Dahl

Favourite animal: Dogs and puppies, of course

Favourite jewellery: A ring engraved with the word 'Love', originally given to her mom Tish by her dad Billy Ray, and a charm bracelet her mom made

Favourite time of day: 1 a.m

Favourite season: Summer

Siblings: Older half-brother Trace and older half-sister Brandi (both on Tish's side), half-brother Christopher Cody Cyrus, younger brother Braison Chance and younger sister Noah Lindsey

Best friends: Tory Sparkman, Emily Osment, Lesley Patterson and her mom, Tish

Godparents: Miley is the goddaughter of country music star and *Hannah Montana* guest star Dolly Parton

Favourite sport: Cheerleading

Favourite topic of conversatio Music and boys

Mobile phone: iPhone

Celebrity crushes: Chad Micha Murray, Ryan Cabrera

Favourite colour: Seafoam gree

Favourite flower: Lavender

in: Franklin, Tennessee, USA
ently living: Between Los
geles, California, USA and a
0-acre farm in Nashville,
nnessee, USA
ents: Singer/actor Billy Ray
rus and Leticia 'Tish' Finley
rus

First big spend: A Coach handbag
Ticklish: YES!
Has a fear of: Spiders
Being a prankster: Miley is known for it
Hidden talent:
Doing a monkey voice
Bad habit: Biting her nails

Favourite boardgame: Trouble
Favourite computer game:
Guitar Hero
Favourite TV shows: *Laguna Beach* and *The Suite Life of Zack and Cody*
Favourite children's story:
The Little Ballerina
Favourite book: *Don't Die, My Love* by Lurlene McDaniel

Favourite sweets: Starburst, Gummy Bears, Peach Rings, and Dots
Favourite cereals: Lucky Charms or a bowl of oatmeal with two scoops of ice cream on top
For dinner: Miley likes to make vegetarian food but doesn't eat anything green

Favourite sound: Rain hitting the ground
Favourite smell: Vanilla
Favourite actor: Orlando Bloom
Favourite actress: Jennifer Anniston
Favourite movie: *Steel Magnolias*
Favourite music: Kelly Clarkson's album *Breakaway*

Introducing
Ms Miley Ray Cyrus

'Miley is smart, funny and totally cute'

WOW! What a year it has been for Miley Ray Cyrus. Her show *Hannah Montana* has become a smash-hit series on the Disney Channel; she has released bestselling music albums both as Miley Ray Cyrus and *Hannah Montana*; has performed at her sell-out tours and is about to start shooting her own *Hannah Montana* movie set for release in 2009.

Not to mention Miley is smart, funny and totally cute. No wonder every girl wants to be Hannah/Miley and live the amazing double-life dream.

Miley's success has shown once and for all that the girl rocks. Not only is she seen at the hottest premières in town, looking fabulous on the red carpet in the coolest of clothes and the most gorgeous of shoes, she has also guest-presented at the 2008 Grammys and the 2008 Oscars and has won numerous awards herself. Plus she has constant access to Hannah Montana's revolving wardrobe. What more could a girl wish for?

With her demand and popularity on the up, the future is looking mighty fine for Hollywood's singing and acting TV darling. But where did it all begin for Hannah Montana and Miley Ray Cyrus?

Early Days

A star was born on the day Destiny Hope Cyrus – Miley's birth name – came into the world on 23 November 1992. That's how her dad Billy Ray Cyrus tells it. At the time, he was wearing a long ponytail, and people all over the country were line dancing to his massive hit, a catchy song called 'Achy Breaky Heart'. His little girl was named Destiny Hope because Billy Ray knew that as soon as he saw his new daughter, her destiny was to bring hope to the world.

With Billy Ray's career in full flight, he took little Destiny out on the road with him: wherever he went, his family came too, just like the characters in *Hannah Montana*. Out on the tour bus, Destiny was given to smiling a lot and quickly earned the nickname 'Smiley'. The name stuck and later it was shortened to 'Miley' – now it's only her grandmother that still calls her by the name Destiny. In 2008 Miley officially changed her name from Destiny to Miley and chose Ray for her new middle name because she wanted to share her dad's name. Cute!

Family Life

It could have been a crazy time for the Cyrus family with Billy Ray's career going from strength to strength and being out on the road so much, but strong ties have always kept them totally together, and that's something Miley still relies on now she has moved into the spotlight. 'Some people don't have a family to fall back on, like I have. That's what keeps me strong,' says Miley.

And what a family. Billy Ray Cyrus met Leticia 'Tish' Finley and they married secretly on 28 December 1992. The household was full of children including Miley's half-brother Christopher Cody, Billy Ray's adopted stepchildren Trace and

MILEY moments

Miley's grandmother is the only person who still calls her by her birth name, Destiny.

9

Brandi, Miley and her younger brother Braison and her little sister Noah.

All of the kids get on really well, but having younger brothers and sisters means there is always something funny happening in the house. Braison takes after his older sis and is a total prankster like Miley. Once he put a wooden snake in Miley's bed. Did she jump! And Miley's six-year-old sister, Noah, sheepishly told her that she had entered a contest on the Disney Channel website to win backstage passes to a concert featuring the network's newest star. It was Miley! 'You live with me! Don't even think about swiping anything from my bedroom to sell on eBay,' Miley told her sister.

On the Ranch

The Cyrus family lived an idyllic life on their farm in Nashville, Tennessee, and Miley had a childhood that most of us can only dream of. She had lots of animals to play with as there was plenty of room for the typical assortment of farm pets: horses, dogs, cats, chickens and fish. Out on the ranch Miley started riding horses when she was only two years old and used to enjoy braiding all of the ponies' tails. In fact, that's what she says she misses the most about the family's move away from the farm.

MILEY moments

Miley is known for playing pranks on people.

HANNAH highs

The *Hannah Montana* soundtrack was the first ever TV soundtrack to debut at No. 1 in the US pop charts, selling 281,000 copies in its first week!

Day to Day Living for a Teen Rock Star

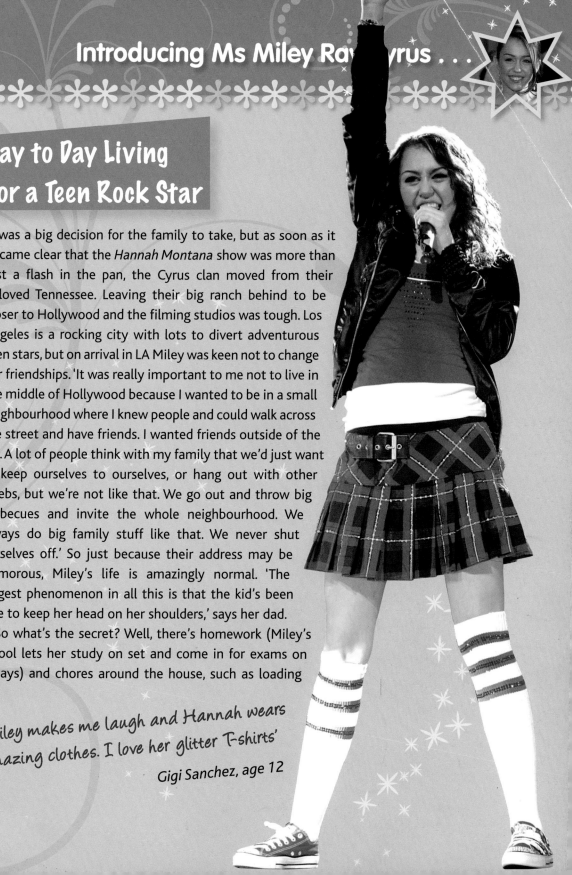

It was a big decision for the family to take, but as soon as it became clear that the *Hannah Montana* show was more than just a flash in the pan, the Cyrus clan moved from their beloved Tennessee. Leaving their big ranch behind to be closer to Hollywood and the filming studios was tough. Los Angeles is a rocking city with lots to divert adventurous teen stars, but on arrival in LA Miley was keen not to change her friendships. 'It was really important to me not to live in the middle of Hollywood because I wanted to be in a small neighbourhood where I knew people and could walk across the street and have friends. I wanted friends outside of the set. A lot of people think with my family that we'd just want to keep ourselves to ourselves, or hang out with other celebs, but we're not like that. We go out and throw big barbecues and invite the whole neighbourhood. We always do big family stuff like that. We never shut ourselves off.' So just because their address may be glamorous, Miley's life is amazingly normal. 'The biggest phenomenon in all this is that the kid's been able to keep her head on her shoulders,' says her dad.

So what's the secret? Well, there's homework (Miley's school lets her study on set and come in for exams on Fridays) and chores around the house, such as loading

'Miley makes me laugh and Hannah wears amazing clothes. I love her glitter T-shirts'

Gigi Sanchez, age 12

Introducing Ms Miley Ray Cyrus . . .

'Miley has the coolest adventures but Hannah has the coolest shoes. Her life is exciting. I wish I could sing like her'

Sophia Strinati, age 11

the dishwasher every night. And every Sunday Miley must attend church with the rest of the family.

Then there are Miley's mom's talks about the mistakes of some young Hollywood stars. 'It is so scary as a mom to see all these kids who are so whacked now,' says Tish. 'I have less freedom than most of my friends,' says Miley. 'I probably have an earlier curfew than anyone just because my mom wants to keep me really safe.'

Miley's mom has other methods of keeping Miley's feet on the ground too. 'My mom knows I love Beyoncé, and she brings me every article on her. She's like, "Look, she's so humble, but she's still amazing".'

If Mom is the family's disciplinarian, Dad is the confidant. 'We're really close,' says Miley. 'I feel like I can tell my dad anything. When we come home, we forget that we even work together and just hang out.'

'No one messes with me and my family. Even working with my dad every day doesn't bother me. When we're at home, it's strictly family! We don't ever bring work home with us because I still need a dad. I don't always want a co-worker, you know what I mean?'

MILEY moments

'I'm always on the computer. I'm a computer nerd!' admits Miley.

Early Signs of Talent

'My dad says I could sing before I could talk, if that's possible. I was always humming and things like that,' says Miley, and it was true as she was singing on the stage with her dad at the tender age of two years old. 'I would sing "Hound Dog" and silly songs for the fun of it.'

And this lack of stage fright has stayed with her, although she does admit to still getting nervous sometimes when playing to large crowds as Hannah Montana. 'When I was little, I would stand up on couches and say, "Watch me". We had these showers that are completely glass, and I would lock people in them and make them stay in there and watch me perform.'

Miley started performing and singing properly at the age of six and wanted to get into show business after visiting the set of a sitcom that her dad was acting in.

But it wasn't all plain sailing. She says that her most embarrassing moment was when she was trying out for her school's dance team. She was practising in the hallway but fell and ripped her denim skirt!

HANNAH highs

HANNAH highs

The name Hannah Montana was changed a few times before it was decided upon. Close seconds were Anna Cabana, Samantha York and Alexis Texas.

Landing the Role of a Lifetime

Having been firmly bitten by the singing and acting bug from an early age, Miley decided to go for it and audition for a role in a new sitcom Disney were putting together. 'As soon as I read the script I knew it kinda related to me. I wanted to disguise myself as not some celebrity's daughter, just be me and find people that like me for me.'

The new show was based around the story of a 14-year-old girl who leads a double life as an international singing sensation. Living in Malibu with her widowed father and older brother, the character seeks to live a normal life and disguises herself from her fans and the paparazzi by wearing a signature blonde wig. The original idea for the show was from a *That's*

MILEY moments

Miley says: 'I'm not letting any stupid decisions get in my way. I want to be a role model, letting girls know that they can follow their dreams.'

So Raven episode in which a child star of a popular TV show would try her hand at going to a normal school. Lots of names were considered but the working title was *The Secret Life of Zoe Stewart*.

Miley's One in a Thousand

The title of the new series was still not confirmed when auditions began with a vengeance, and more than a thousand young actresses put their name forward for the ultimate teen role. It was a massive gamble for Miley as, being only 11 years old and the character being 14 years old, she was very young. But boy, when Miley wants something, she will try as hard as Hannah Montana to get it. And so her adventure really began.

'I love Hannah's acting and singing. She is so talented'

Becky Palmer, age 13

Best of Both Worlds

Lights, Camera, Auditions!

MILEY first auditioned for the new Disney show *Zoe Stewart*. 'The audition process for anything is so scary,' Miley says. 'You walk into a room with sixty girls. In my case, I have to say, if I was them I don't know why they chose me. You can see their head shots and just know they know a lot more than you do. They don't like you – that is the scariest part! I did taping. I did two tapes, four tapes. I started out as Lilly and they wanted me to audition for the main role and that sounded very positive. But they said, "You are too small, too young. Bye-bye." Well, that's rude. So I made another tape. Dang it! They are going to watch my tape and like it!'

The main character was a year older than Miley and comments were made that she was just too small to pull it off. Joanna 'JoJo' Levesque was offered the title role but turned it down – luckily for all us Hannah fans.

Landing the Dream Role

It was a really hard slog for Miley to convince the show's producers that she was right for the job. 'I auditioned forever. At first they said I was too small and too young. But afterwards I was like "One more time? I can dress up differently! I can look older!" So I kept trying out and it was still no, so I freaked out.'

But it was the determination and experience learned by watching her dad that kept her going. 'We went out [to California] and I auditioned one more time, and I got the part,' she says. 'I had lost my teeth before the audition, my front teeth, four of them, had braces on top. Even though I

22

talk a lot, my mouth and face is tiny. I was sitting there with huge buck teeth and huge braces and huge hair and tiny little body. But four months later the show's producers were like "Come to California".'

What ultimately won Miley the job, the producers and network executives say, was her cool confidence, intuitive comic timing and a husky singing voice. And into the bargain, Miley, who sings the show's theme song, was able to infuse Hannah with a real-life sense of the joys and perils of superstardom.

Miley's life and the life of her family and friends were about to change forever, but no one had any idea just exactly how much.

HANNAH highs

Hannah Montana likes hot dogs and cheetos in her dressing room.

Hannah Montana Early Success

'I love Hannah's clothes and the way she puts on her make-up'

April Rose, age 14

Filmed at Tribune Studios in Hollywood, with the very cool setting of Malibu Beach (with its own sand), *Hannah Montana* debuted on the Disney Channel on 24 March 2006. It was meant to have 22 episodes in its first season, but due to popular demand a further four episodes were added. It was a huge hit as soon as it aired, attracting 5.4 million viewers in the US, the highest rating for a Disney TV show ever.

And the success keeps on growing. The show now reaches over 164 million viewers worldwide – and is translated into six different languages – and is ranked the No.1 kids' series for six to 14 year olds.

HANNAH highs

In *The Simpsons* episode 'Eternal Moonshine of the Simpson Mind', Bart writes (on the blackboard) 'The capital of Montana is not Hannah'.

Miley's Favourite Place On Set

With the tough but exciting filming schedule and scripts to learn, on-set relationships are all important. Having been put together by a team of producers, the show's set and co-stars have started to feel like home for Miley – with a few added extras – and she has her own special places to hang out. 'It used to be my dressing room, but I also love the beach set because it's really cool, but your shoes get really dirty and disgusting. It's dirty, but it's kinda fun to feel like you're on the beach.'

'There's nothing like being on a set where you are there to make other people happy and to make them laugh. It's the best job in the world! Sometimes it can be frustrating to have a camera on you all the time, because if you do something

MILEY moments

Miley says: 'Pink isn't just a colour, it's an attitude!'

embarrassing or make a mistake, everyone will know about it. Sometimes my friends will call and tease me about something they saw, and I just have to laugh and say "Thanks guys, I love you too!"'

And it's not just her friends who give Miley a gentle teasing; her dad and co-stars get in on the act too. Miley says: 'When we're doing photo shoots or something, Dad'll just yell out random things that I wouldn't want anyone to know – "Remember when you were a kid?" kind of stuff. But it's funny. It breaks the ice and makes everyone smile. If it takes some embarrassing me to make everyone happy, I'll take it.' But Billy Ray is sure to give his daughter some space. Even though they occupy adjoining alcoves on the sound stage, they are separated by a frilly curtain. He is definitely one cool Dad.

MILEY moments

Miley says she likes the fans. 'It's cool to know people support you.'

Being Hannah Montana

So what's it like acting out the part of the most famous teen star in the world? 'I've always loved singing, and I've always loved acting and dancing,' says Miley. 'Getting this opportunity with Disney, I get to do it all. They let you do everything you love.'

'It all starts from the root of it, which is the show. And that's showing a normal girl that also has this huge dream and she's getting to live it ... And everyone has that. I think no

matter whether it's for singing or acting or whatever you want to do, everyone has that dream that they want to go for.'

And that's why we love her. Miley and Hannah are total role models – they represent both the reality and the dream. The dream we all have to be famous and be a popstar.

But it's not just all about role models; Miley loves her alter ego because of her fabulous wardrobe too! 'Playing Hannah is a total girl thing. It's like dressing up every day.'

So Hannah or Miley?

Playing such different characters means it must be hard for a young actress to choose which she prefers, but Miley is clear: 'I relate more to the Miley character because that's kind of how I am when I am not working. We go and get ice cream down the street. I like my Miley Stewart life, and when I go to the set I definitely feel like I am living the script.'

And she is living the script in lots of ways as Miley's own singing career has taken off and Miley Stewart's friends have become her very own.

'Hannah's hair and clothes are amazing. Pink is my favourite colour and I think we have a lot in common. I want to be Hannah!'

Anna Valentine, age 11

30

Hannah Montana Co-stars

Emily Osment

Every big TV character needs a great best friend, and Miley Stewart is very lucky to have the hilarious Lilly Truscott as a trusted sidekick. Emily Osment plays loveable Lilly and her multicolour-haired alter ego Lola. Since the moment they first met on set, a real friendship developed between the girls and they've been best friends from that moment.

Emily has had a long career in Hollywood showbiz, having first been cast in commercials, then landing her first acting role in *The Secret Life of Girls* at the tender age of seven. Since then she has worked with Glenn Close and on TV shows like *Touched by an Angel*, *Friends* and *3rd Rock from the Sun*. Before *Hannah Montana* she was most famous for her roles of Gerti Giggles in the *Spy Kids* trilogy.

The amazing success of *Hannah Montana* took everyone by surprise, not least Emily: 'I had no idea the show would be so big. At first I thought "Oh, this might be cute." Then when we did the pilot everybody was saying how big

they thought it was gonna be – I was like "yeah, right, whatever", but now it's really happening and I was caught by surprise!' She explains: 'Now when we go out I get recognised a lot, especially if I'm with Miley – there's always lots of kids staring at us!'

When they are not together Miley and Emily are constantly texting or conference calling each other. They share everything, including their talents and their friends: Miley has helped Emily learn to play guitar and Emily has taught Miley how to knit. And Miley and Emily both hang out with Vanessa Hudgens and the stars of *The Suite Life of Zack and Cody*, Brenda Song and Ashley Tisdale. Pretty cool.

Mitchel Musso

The *Hannah Montana* friendship circle wouldn't be complete without experienced actor and all-round action guy Mitchel Musso who plays Oliver Oken. Growing up in Texas with his brothers, Mitchel followed his older brother into the acting profession. He has appeared in films and TV series including *Secondhand Lions*, with – by coincidence – Emily Osment's brother Haley Joel Osment. He also appeared in a Disney movie called *Life is Ruff* and alongside Chuck Norris in *Walker Texas Ranger*, but he is best known for his great one-liners and excellent hair in *Hannah Montana*.

But Mitchel is not just a pretty face with great acting skills, he has his own rap album in the works and some songs are already recorded and up on YouTube to hear. His role in *Hannah Montana* has been a great joy and an amazing ride. Not only has he made some of his best friends ever, he has also found some other plus points. 'My favourite thing the show has given me is the fans. I love having fans! That's my favourite thing, for people to come up and ask for an

'Hair helps me with confidence. I can be preppy, I can be punky, I can pretty much do every look'

autograph. It's all about them and they're there for you!'

So, from Seasons One and Two which episode is his favourite? Surprisingly it's 'O Say Can You Remember the Words'. 'But I also had to do the most embarrassing thing in that episode, which was sing. I was so scared to sing in front of everybody. That was like the worst fear I've had in my entire life!' Luckily he had some moral support on set: 'Miley's been my best friend for like two years, so it's really easy going to work everyday with your best friend.'

MITCHEL MUSSO FACTS!

Born: Mitchel Tate Musso on 9 July 1991

Height: 5ft 8in

Interests: Acting, basketball, skateboarding, listening to his iPod, hanging out with friends

Favourite movie: *The Matrix*

Favourite music: He likes hip-hop and rock music. His favourite bands are Queen, Metro Station, Blink 182 and Fall Out Boy

Favorite song: 'Disco!' by Metro Station

Favourite dessert: Coffee ice cream

Favourite TV show: *American Idol*

Jason Earles

JASON EARLES FACTS!

born: Jason Daniel Earles in San Diego, California, USA on 26 April (the year is still a mystery)

height: 5ft 3in

eyes: Blue

hidden talent: Jason is a trained Shakespearean actor

pets: Two cats called Timmy and Presley

favourite music: Coldplay, The Fray and Death Cab for Cutie

favourite cartoon: *South Park*

Playing an annoying brother came pretty easy to Jason Earles. He loved the script of the show as soon as he read it and wanted to become Jackson Rod Stewart and have some fun. Laid back and casual, Jackson is typically the comic relief of the series, using one-liners or calling Miley names and tormenting her with his big brother antics and slapstick schemes.

Given excellent comic situations against his 'frenemy' Rico (Moises Arias), he says: 'My favourite part of the set is Rico's Surf Shack. They built it sort of as my set, as a place for Jackson to work so you could set up a whole bunch of storylines from there.'

'Moises is one of my favourite characters that they've added,' Jason says. 'A tiny little pint-size guy and for some reason he's always in a position of authority over me, and it's like he takes the greatest pleasure in making me miserable and it ends up being really funny.'

But his training at classical acting school was far from Malibu Beach. Appearing in many highbrow plays and movies including *National Treasure*, he is now best known for his role as an honorary Cyrus sibling. 'I was really nervous when I first found out Billy Ray was going to be the dad. They've got all this history and get each other, and I am going to be the outsider. But they are classic Southern hospitality. It took me all of two days to feel accepted. They gave me Ray as a middle name. Everybody has Ray for a middle name.'

'I was surprised at how close everybody on set got, so quickly – the group got really tight, like by the end of the pilot! All the kids were swapping numbers and hanging out at each other's houses and hanging out before it was actually picked up [by the network]. Almost to the point where you become a family that you have the little bickering stuff. But then you always make up!'

Billy Ray Cyrus

So, what's it like playing Robby Ray Stewart, a fictional character that is not so loosely based on his own relationship with his daughter? Pretty good by all accounts! 'Miley's been my best friend for the past two years, so it's really easy-going on the set working with your best friend. The whole cast is just as close off set as they are on set. We all kind of became a big old family and best friends. It's awesome.'

As Hannah's dad, Robby manages Hannah Montana's career and writes most of Hannah's songs. He provides a wise voice both on and off set but doesn't mind a little teasing. Long hair on men was big in country music in the early nineties and Billy Ray had the mullet of all mullets (that's short on top and the sides and long at the back). On the show he has a laugh at his own expense – singing songs like 'I Want My Mullet Back' and even impersonating himself, Billy Ray Cyrus, by wearing a long mullet wig on the show – showing what a great sense of humour he has.

Perhaps that's where Miley got her excellent sense of fun from. The relationship they share is more than father and daughter. As Billy Ray says: 'I've always tried to be her best friend; on *Hannah Montana* it's really life imitating art imitating life.' Sure, so much so that Miley's least favourite part of working with her dad is the car drive up to the studio. So embarrassing.

BILLY RAY CYRUS FACTS!

born: William Ray Cyrus on 25 August 1961 in Flatwoods, Kentucky

height: 6ft

early success: 'Achy Breaky Heart' made line dancing popular again

tv surprises: He appeared on *Dancing with the Stars*, the US version of *Strictly Come Dancing*

Guest Appearances

With the hit TV show going from strength to strength, many actors and singing stars have appeared in Seasons One and Two of the show. Corbin Bleu, of *High School Musical* fame, made an excellent cameo appearance as the drop-dead handsome Johnny Collins and discovered the wonders of ketchup; Dolly Parton visits the set often to play her role as Aunt Dolly; Ashley Tisdale appeared as Maddie Fitzpatrick; Brooke Shields starred as Miley and Jackson's mother in a dream sequence; and the Rock played, well, himself ... with a little added make-up and nail varnish!

The Gorgeous Cody Linley

Playing the *Hannah Montana* character Jake Ryan, Cody Linley almost broke Miley's heart. Luckily Miley and Jake are friends and they both learned a lesson about normal life versus the celebrity lifestyle. But even though his character is in and out of the show, Cody's appearance did mean that Miley had her first on-screen kiss with the hottie teen star. And it's hard to forget those gorgeous looks and winning smile. No wonder her character was upset when he went off to film in Europe and then dated her pop star rival.

Cody had acted before in lots of movies and TV shows – some even with Emily Osment – but: 'Before *Hannah Montana*, I didn't really get recognised a lot. Every once in a while people would come up to me and say, "Have you been in a movie because I swear I've seen you somewhere." But now I'll have people come up to me. It's almost always a girl and sometimes it's crazy. I went to my ex-girlfriend's school's football game and literally there were fifty people chasing us and screaming and trying to take pictures. It was really weird. That's when I was like, "Jeez, *Hannah Montana* is a really popular show".'

And how right Cody is. The popularity spilled over from the screen to live appearances and finally to Miley staging a huge American tour as Hannah Montana. A wild ride was ahead for Miley Ray.

CODY LINLEY FACTS!

born: 20 November 1989
hair colour: Naturally brown, but he dyed it blond for the movie *Hoot*
height: 5ft 7in
favourite music: Country and rock
favourite pizza: Hawaiian
hidden talent: Beat-boxing

'I like a girl who laughs a lot. That's my main thing. If we have fun together then she's for me! If a girl can make me smile then I'll want to kiss her'

Hannah Montana Live

'I love all the
glitter and
the diamonds'

Stepping into the Lights

With so much success in the studio and on TV, it seemed a
natural move for Hannah Montana to meet her fans at live
concert tours. As Miley said: 'Acting is a big part of my life. But
I'm very excited for the tour, getting out there. The thirty
minutes on stage – it's the best thirty minutes ever. Looking
at the crowd, seeing their faces and hearing them say the
positive words of the songs, it's really important for me.'

And, boy, was it a tight turnaround from the end of
shooting Season Two to beginning the preparations for her
tour. 'We finished shooting the last episode of *Hannah
Montana* and then the very next day I woke up nine a.m,
started running with a trainer and had to get into
rehearsals. It's been great though, I feel so good, not just
physically from being fit and being on tour, but also
mentally.'

The Show's on the Road

'Getting ready for the show is a lot of fun but a lot
of hard work,' says Miley, as there were dance
routines to learn, songs to remember and screaming

'I love all the
glitter and
the diamonds'

Miley once sang in a Starbucks to get money for a coffee!

HANNAH highs

'Just Like You' and 'The Other Side of Me' were originally tested for the opening theme song for *Hannah Montana*, before 'Best of Both Worlds' was chosen.

crowds to entertain.

But she was in safe hands. The concert tour was choreographed, created and directed by Kenny Ortega, the director and choreographer of *High School Musical*, *High School Musical 2* and *The Cheetah Girls 2*.

And putting the band together was an easy part for the *Hannah Montana* team as it's headed up by Miley's sister Brandi, on lead electric guitar. Due to Miley's crazy filming schedule, the two girls use this touring time as a great way of catching up. Miley says: 'The one person in the world who could keep my deepest secrets is probably my big sister,' so they are very close.

It really is a family affair as Miley's mom is always with her on tour, as is Brandi. But Billy Ray stays behind to look after the ranch. 'He's actually never been on the road with me. Which is, like, totally crazy. I was kind of bummin',' says Miley. 'He came for a couple of shows, but he takes care of my little sister and my animals.'

We All Want Tickets

There was no surprise that demand for precious concerts tickets would be high, but even the organisers were shocked by just how big the demand to see the girls was. Every concert across America was a sell-out, with some tickets later being sold on for thousands of dollars. Miley even ended up extending her *Best of Both Worlds* tour, with over 14 extra performances after all 55 shows were sold out in minutes. It was the most in-demand concert ticket of 2007, and one dollar of each ticket went to benefit the City of Hope Foundation, which helps in the fight against cancer.

We Can All Go to the Concert

Starring Miley Cyrus, the Jonas Brothers, Kenny Ortega and Billy Ray Cyrus, the 3-D version of Miley's *Best of Both Worlds* concert debuted in only 683 cinemas worldwide on Super Bowl Weekend in January 2008. It beat all the other films being shown (which were playing in a larger number of theatres) with a record-breaking $31 million in just its first weekend. Hannah really does rock.

The film was released in Brazil on 29 February 2008, in the UK on 14 March 2008 and in Australia on 20 March 2008, and was greeted with a fantastic response from fans. They queued around the block for tickets to the film, and because of its huge success there are possible plans for a Disney DVD release in Summer 2008. Fingers crossed!

The film shows Miley Cyrus on her *Best of Both Worlds* tour as Hannah Montana, with film clips taken from her performance in Salt Lake City, Utah. Combining documentary elements and behind-the-scenes clips, we get to see the backstage conversion from Hannah Montana to Miley Cyrus, and the buzzing atmosphere of the production.

Out From the Shadows

The *Hannah Montana* tour has been great and Miley has loved every minute, but she can't wait to step out from under the wig and perform for her fans: 'I can't wait to be known as Miley Cyrus the singer. Disney thought it would be great if not only Hannah Montana was a singer, but Miley Cyrus was as well. They've been talking about having Hannah Montana open for Miley Cyrus and for us to do concerts together.' We can only hope that will happen some time soon.

FAVOURITE SONGS TO PERFORM

'I Got Nerve' – the theme of her show

'See You Again' as everyone sings along with that song

'I like Hannah Montana because she's a role model popstar. She is great'

Mia Fry, age 11

43

Fame

Best friend
Tory: 'Miley's so
good about our
friendship and she
makes such an
effort. She rocks'

Don't Go Changin'

WHEN she's out on tour Miley deals so well with her fame and keeps her feet firmly on the ground – even in the Hannah heels! – by travelling not just with her family but taking some friends along too. And there is a definite upside travelling on the *Hannah Montana* tour: Miley's friends get to keep some of Hannah's clothes after they've been worn only once. Can you imagine going crazy in that wardrobe? Lucky friends.

The Fame Game

And perhaps this is why Miley is so popular: what you see is what you get. She's a genuine person who hasn't let it all go to her head.

Recently Miley was asked how she deals with being famous. Modest as ever, she said: 'I don't know how I deal with it – maybe from watching my dad, because he takes everything one step at a time, that's what he taught me too, don't get so wrapped in what's going on that you can't bring yourself back to reality. Whenever I do feel myself just getting all caught up in what's going on, and maybe

MILEY HIGH SUCCESS

★ 'Outstanding Female Lead in a Comedy Series (Child or Adolescent)' at the 2008 Gracie Allen Awards

★ 'Choice TV Actress in a Comedy' at the 2007 Teen Choice Awards

★ 'Choice Summer Artist' at the 2007 Teen Choice Awards

★ 'Favourite TV Actress' at the 2007 Kid's Choice Awards

'I have always been known as Billy Ray Cyrus's daughter. Now they say my name. I freak out!'

getting stuck in the little box I've been put in, I try to do something to bring me out of the box and make me different and make me not just be another girl on TV, but be able to relate to everyone I'm with too.'

Star Spotting

And it's not always easy being the biggest teen star in the world. Sometimes she gets caught without her make-up on and is worried she'll scare her fans away. One time: 'I went to Universal [Studios, Hollywood theme park] with my brother and a friend. The recognition was immediate. It was craziness – all the kids on every ride. I felt like I was going to hurl after one ride, and all the kids were like, "Hannah Montana is about to puke!"' Now, that's a private moment!

A Role Model

Miley is truly a unique star because she takes real responsibility for her fans and for the fame that comes with this dream job. She wants to be a great role model for girls everywhere and has established some Miley rules: 'I say what I'm comfortable in and what I like and nothing that's too out there. I like to look kind of like what girls would want to look up to.'

Fans are Tops

So, what has all this success and fame taught the teenager? 'Know your place, know how you're blessed. That's what I've really learned, that the fans are everything.' And when asked what's the best part about being so successful at such a young age, she says: 'I think that you have more opportunities to grow. You don't get stuck in one type of film or whatever you are doing. As you grow, all the different things that you do can grow with you.'

R.E.S.P.E.C.T and Miley Has It

It's great to know, in a world of crazy celebrity and with some young pop stars going off the rails, that Miley is everything we would hope her to be. She's kind to her millions of fans and knows that they have made her dream possible. She even wants to make friends with them: 'I care so much about my fans. I'll be at my meet-and-greets and I'll see girls my age. I'm like, "Mom, can you get those girls' numbers so we can hang out on the bus afterward?" My mom's like, "Miley, you can't do that".'

Maybe one day we'll be invited back to the tour bus to look through Hannah's wardrobe. Now that would be cool ...

The Look

Miley's Got It All

WITH her amazing looks, her fantastic long hair and a smile that lights up stadiums, we all want to know the secret of Miley's effortless style. Like everything in her life, Miley seems to take it easy and enjoys both the dressing up and dressing down of pop star living.

Comfort Versus Cool

'I think from having to dress up on the show so much, on my days off or in the studio I like being as comfy as possible. My style is very comfy-casual. Sometimes I like to put on jeans, a white T-shirt and cute boots, and sometimes I like being in little Juicy sweats – it depends on my mood.'

MILEY'S FAVOURITE SHOPS

Nordstrom
Target
Intuition (hip LA
 store)
Juicy Couture
American Apparel
Free People
Urban Outfitters
bebe
Abercrombie & Fitch
Aéropostle
Uncle Sam's
Miss Sixty
Limited Too
Diesel

Miley's Make-up

'I love playing dress-up with my little sister, Noah. It's so much fun to sit there and do her make-up!'

With her natural good looks, Miley needs to apply hardly any make-up, but she's a girl's girl and enjoys looking good. She is never out of the house without her lip gloss and loves the brand MAC: 'I love so many of their colours. I guess I pick out the more natural ones, pinky ones or dusty rose. I like fooling around with different colours.'

Miley Stylin'

Although Miley credits her mom for much of her excellent wardrobe, like any top TV star Miley has her own stylist. Her name is Tara Sweenen and, boy, would we all like to share her! At her recent appearance at the Grammys, Miley looked totally stunning.

So, how does a stylist work out what to dress their clients in? Tina says that her starting point was Miley's new darker hair: 'It's still sort of a drastic change, especially from the blonde Hannah Montana,' she says, 'so we're trying to lighten things up for her major red-carpet events.' Hence the amazing white Celine dress with dreamy sparkles. 'Obviously she really likes sequins – she is fifteen!'

But that doesn't mean that she won't be trying

'It usually takes me up to two hours to get ready for a big party, but recently I only had thirty minutes to throw stuff on and I still managed it'

more sophisticated looks. Tina recently said that Miley 'likes to rock out and try new things', and that we can expect to see more of an edge in her clothing choices, taking cues from style icons like Ashlee Simpson. 'She's a rock star, and that's what we're going to see a lot more of this year.' We can't wait.

Shopping Shopping Shopping

With only a reported $300 allowance per month, Miley likes to find a bargain like the rest of us. But she does splurge – Miley and her younger sister were recently spotted shopping after one of her sell-out concerts in LA at a Beverly Hills boutique.

But it's not all high-end clothing stores. Like any sane teenager, Miley loves to hang out at the mall with friends and go shopping. But she does have her eye on a special shopping buddy or two: 'I'd like to go shopping with Ashley Tisdale – she has the best style. If I could go shopping with someone I haven't met, I'd love to go shopping with Beyoncé: it's like everything is bling all the time. Everything is diamonds and jewels.' That would be a fun trip to join in on.

'I love tube socks. Everyone's like, what's with those socks? But that's my style'

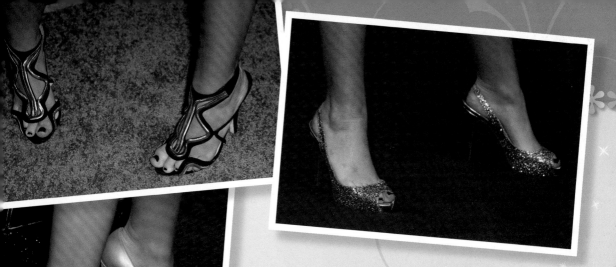

Shoes Glorious Shoes

It's a passion, and after a quick look inside Hannah Montana's wardrobe we can only guess how big Miley's shoe collection is. 'I'm a big shoe person. Sometimes I'll be punky, the next day I'll be preppy. Every day after work my mom and I go shopping. My dad is about to kill me, but I say "We need it Daddy!"'

Steal Miley's Style!

Top tips from Miley's stylist:
To get Miley's classic but funky look, try pairing your favourite slim leg blue jeans with a plain white puff sleeve tunic top. Throw on a comfortable pair of brown slouchy boots and curl the ends of your hair into soft waves. To liven up this simple outfit, add a few colourful bangles and a few simple pieces of gold jewellery (don't go overboard, Miley never does). Throw on some big sunglasses, a soft, slouchy handbag and a lick of lip gloss and you're ready to meet your public.

Hannah's Look

As we know, it's all about sparkles and glitter and strong colours for Hannah's wardrobe, but contrary to popular belief,

MILEY'S FAVOURITE SHOE BRANDS

Converse

Zappos

UGG

Amazon

Nike

'I think of rock, glamour, Hollywood for my style'

Miley's 'Hannah' blonde wig doesn't have its own security guard. Though it does sit on a prosthetic head upon which Miley has drawn a face and called 'Tanya'. The wigs are custom-made to fit Miley perfectly: 'I have two with me on tour and two more back in L.A. They're so, like, valuable, and you have to be super, super easy with them. So we have extra ones, just in case.' And to prevent it from falling, the wig's fringe is glued to Miley Cyrus's forehead. Ouch! Miley does suffer for her art.

HANNAH STYLE FACT

When Disney released a Hannah Montana clothing collection in 2007, Emily Osment helped to design some of the pieces from the range

CREATE YOUR OWN HANNAH STYLE

Your pop star name

Eye colour:

Hair colour:

Style – glitter and pink, or down and denim?

T-shirt colour:

Jacket colour:

Skirt or jeans?

What kind of phone do you use?

Shoes – highs or lows?

Sunglasses or hairclips?

Favourite song:

Favourite dance moves:

Work out your dance routine here

Friendships and Crushes

The Perfect Mr Miley Ray Cyrus

WHEN it comes to love, Miley is as honest as she is in every area of her life. 'I've got high standards when it comes to boys. As my dad says, all girls should! I'm from the American South and down there we're all about southern hospitality. I know that if I like a guy, he'd better be nice, and, above all, my dad has to approve of him!'

PERFECT BOYFRIEND

Must have lots of personality

Must make Miley laugh

Must be calm

Must love music

Say What?!

As Miley's fame has increased, the press has been full of rumours about Miley and Nick Jonas, of Jonas Brothers fame. Some journalists wrote that they had started dating on the *Best of Both Worlds* tour, but Miley has denied the relationship. There were reports that they split in December 2007 but, plain talking as ever, Miley said they weren't together in the first place, so how could they

have broken up?! A good point, but interest is high in this pretty young star and her personal life looks set to appear in future gossip columns, just like Hannah's on the show. So far, though, we've only seen Miley Stewart's kisses.

Kissing and Crushes

Like any girl would, Miley recently confessed that she really enjoyed her on-screen kiss with co-star Cody Linley: 'I think he's cute! I have a total crush on him but he doesn't like me, but I don't care because he's so much fun to look at. I love being on set with him. He's a really cool guy. He's really fun and down to earth and he's hot! The kissing scene was my favourite scene all season! It was a perfect kiss. His lips are

like velvet.' Good to know. But she didn't have quite the same experience kissing co-star Rico: 'Well I had to kiss Moises and I was like, "Guys, this is seriously not fair. You owe me no kissing scenes for a month unless it's Cody Linley!"'

A Forward Flip

Miley admits she's been known to be bold when it comes to guys. 'I've done some pretty crazy stuff, but the craziest was probably when I was at summer church camp. I saw this guy and I was like, "Oh my gosh, he's so cute!" He was doing back flips off the diving board, and he said to me that I should try it. I was so nervous – but I just kept telling myself, "Just go, you can do it." So I did, and I did a double back flip! It didn't work out between us, but I proved to myself I could do the flip.'

Slumber Party Secrets

Boys are all well and good, but what Miley really loves is to have slumber parties with her best friends. It's a relaxing time and they get to talk about boys, sing, play games and load up on her favourite snacks of cookie-dough and sweets: 'I'm a girly girl. My friends and I love to chill.'

Miley's bedroom is totally glam and girly, and so it is the perfect place to catch up on gossip and the latest crushes: 'My bedroom

MILEY MOMENTS

Miley's favourite pop singers are Hilary Duff, Kelly Clarkson and Ashlee Simpson.

walls are this cool blue and they've got big metallic circles on them with the words "vogue" and "chic" everywhere. I've got candles and flowers everywhere too because I'm really into yoga. And then I've got these big zebra chairs that are so cool.'

'I'm super lucky to live near my closest friends, Ashley Tisdale and Vanessa Hudgens. Vanessa and I were sleeping over at Ashley's one night. V and I shared one bed and Ash slept in the other.' Oh, to be a fly on the wall there – can you imagine the gossip?!

'I want to be Hannah!'
Lilly Palmer, age 6

Girlfriends Rock

It's nights in with the girls that Miley really appreciates: 'When I was going through a hard time about a boy, my friend spent the night talking to me. She let me talk all night. I just sat there, like, "I miss him".'

'Girlfriends are so important as there is no time for dating right now,' says Miley. 'I'm too busy working to have a boyfriend – I think my dad likes this job because it keeps the boys away.'

So perhaps love is on hold for a while, as Miley's life doesn't look like it is getting any quieter with so many amazing *Hannah Montana* projects on the horizon, and her own singing career taking off.

What's next for Miley and Hannah?

Happy 15th Birthday Miley!

At an amazing birthday party for nearly 15,000 people, Miley sang to her home town Nashville. It was so important for Miley to give something back to the place where it all began, and to tell the world: 'Anyone from a small town can go out there and live their dream.' It's the message that is so strong in everything that Miley does.

The Future Is Bright

And the dream just keeps on going. Recently, Miley has presented awards at the Grammys and the Oscars, she has begun filming her new movie and starts work on *Hannah Montana* Season Three soon.

We Love Miley! We Love Hannah!

So, it's looking good for the amazing, talented Miley Ray Cyrus and her pop-sensation character Hannah. We can only wait for *Hannah Montana* Season Three and the movie in 2009 to enjoy more of this wonderful star.

Miley and Hannah really are best of both girls. xxx

61

Picture Credits

GETTY: 2, 4-5, 6, 7, 8, 9, 10 (bottom left), 11, 14, 15, 17 (bottom right), 18, 21, 24, 30, 35, 41, 44, 45 (top), 46, 47 (top and bottom right), 48, 49, 50, 52 (top and bottom left), 54, 55, 56 (bottom), 57, 58, 59, 63
REX FEATURES: 3, 10 (top), 12, 13, 16, 17 (top and bottom left), 19, 20, 22, 23, 25, 26, 27, 29 (bottom), 31, 32, 33, 37, 38, 39, 40, 42, 43, 47 (top), 51, 56 (top), 60, 61
PA PHOTOS: 28, 29 (top), 36, 46 (bottom), 47 (centre), 52 (top right)

Acknowledgements

Posy Edwards would like to thank Malcolm Edwards, Helia Pheonix, Briony Hartley, Helen Ewing, Anna Valentine, David Jones, Clare Wallis, Kate Oliver, Felix Cole, Max Cole, Angela Pope, Gigi Sanchez and Amanda Harris.

First published in hardback in Great Britain in 2008 by Orion Books
an imprint of the Orion Publishing Group Ltd
Orion House, 5 Upper St Martin's Lane,
London WC2H 9EA
An Hachette Livre UK Company

1 3 5 7 9 10 8 6 4 2

A CIP catalogue record for this book is available from the British Library.

ISBN: 978 1 4091 0075 1

Designed by www.goldustdesign.co.uk
Printed in Canada

The Orion Publishing Group's policy is to use papers that are natural, renewable and recyclable and made from wood grown in sustainable forests. The logging and manufacturing processes are expected to conform to the environmental regulations of the country of origin. Every effort has been made to fulfil requirements with regard to reproducing copyright material. The author and publisher will be glad to rectify any omissions at the earliest opportunity.

www.orionbooks.co.uk